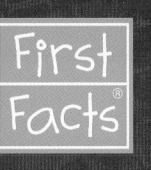

First Facts®

SCIENCE **BASICS**

WHAT IS
FORCE?

by Jody S. Rake

raintree

a Capstone company—publishers for children
www.raintree.co.uk

Raintree is an imprint of Capstone Global Library Limited, a company incorporated in England and Wales having its registered office at 264 Banbury Road, Oxford, OX2 7DY – Registered company number: 6695582

www.raintree.co.uk
myorders@raintree.co.uk

Edited by Jaclyn Jaycox and Mari Bolte
Designed by Kyle Grentz
Original illustrations © Capstone Global Library Limited 2019
Picture research by Eric Gohl
Production by Laura Manthe
Originated by Capstone Global Library Ltd
Printed and bound in India

ISBN 978 1 4747 7083 5 (hardback)   ISBN 978 1 4747 7087 3 (paperback)
23 22 21 20 19   24 23 22 21 20
10 9 8 7 6 5 4 3 2 1   10 9 8 7 6 5 4 3 2 1

British Library Cataloguing in Publication Data
A full catalogue record for this book is available from the British Library.

Acknowledgements
We would like to thank the following for permission to reproduce photographs: AP Photo: John Raoux, 19; Capstone Studio: Karon Dubke, 20–21; Shutterstock: Christina Richards, 17, Drazen Vukelic, 9, Prasit Rodphan, 5, saicle, background (throughout), Samot, 15, Todd Taulman Photography, cover, Vasyl Shulga, 7, xtock, 11.

Every effort has been made to contact copyright holders of material reproduced in this book. Any omissions will be rectified in subsequent printings if notice is given to the publisher.

All the internet addresses (URLs) given in this book were valid at the time of going to press. However, due to the dynamic nature of the internet, some addresses may have changed, or sites may have changed or ceased to exist since publication. While the author and publisher regret any inconvenience this may cause readers, no responsibility for any such changes can be accepted by either the author or the publisher.

CONTENTS

Let the force move you **4**

Science friction **8**

A heavy situation **10**

Electric forces **12**

Using forces **14**

Pushing with thrust **18**

Force experiment **20**

Glossary 22

Find out more 23

Comprehension questions 24

Index 24

LET THE FORCE
MOVE YOU

Force is a push or a pull. Force happens when two objects come together. When you opened this book, you used force to make the cover move. You use forces every day.

Forces make things move. They can also make a moving object stop. When you kick a ball that is sitting still, it moves. When you catch a moving ball, it stops.

Force can also change the speed and direction of a moving object. The faster you pedal your bike, the faster it moves. If you move the handlebars, the bike changes direction.

SCIENCE
FRICTION

There are many types of forces. When you roll a toy car across the floor, it will slow down and stop. The force that makes it stop is called **friction**. Friction happens when one **surface** rubs against another. Friction helps you walk. The force of friction on the ground keeps your foot from sliding.

friction force made when two objects rub
 against each other
surface outside or outermost area
 of something

AIR RESISTANCE

Air has its own kind of friction. Air *resistance* slows down a moving object. The amount of air resistance depends on the size of the surface. A bigger surface will have more air resistance. This is why a large parachute floats gently to the ground. Something smaller and with less air resistance, such as a rock, will fall faster.

FACT

Some surfaces have more friction than others. A toy car will roll further on a wooden floor than it will on carpet. This is because rough carpet has more friction than smooth wood.

resistance force that opposes or slows the motion of an object

A HEAVY
SITUATION

Gravity is a force that pulls two objects together. Earth has gravity. Without gravity, the spinning Earth would fling us off the planet and into space. Gravity gives things weight. Bigger objects usually have more weight because of gravity.

FACT

The weight of an object can change if the amount of gravity changes. The stronger the gravity, the heavier an object will be. Earth has more gravity than the Moon. An astronaut who weighs 82 kilograms (180 pounds) on Earth weighs only 14 kg (30 pounds) on the Moon!

ELECTRIC
FORCES

All things are made of tiny particles called **atoms**. They can have a positive or negative electric charge. An electric force happens between charged atoms. If objects have different charges, they will move closer together. If they have the same charges, they will move away from each other.

atoms tiny particles (pieces) of which
  everything is made

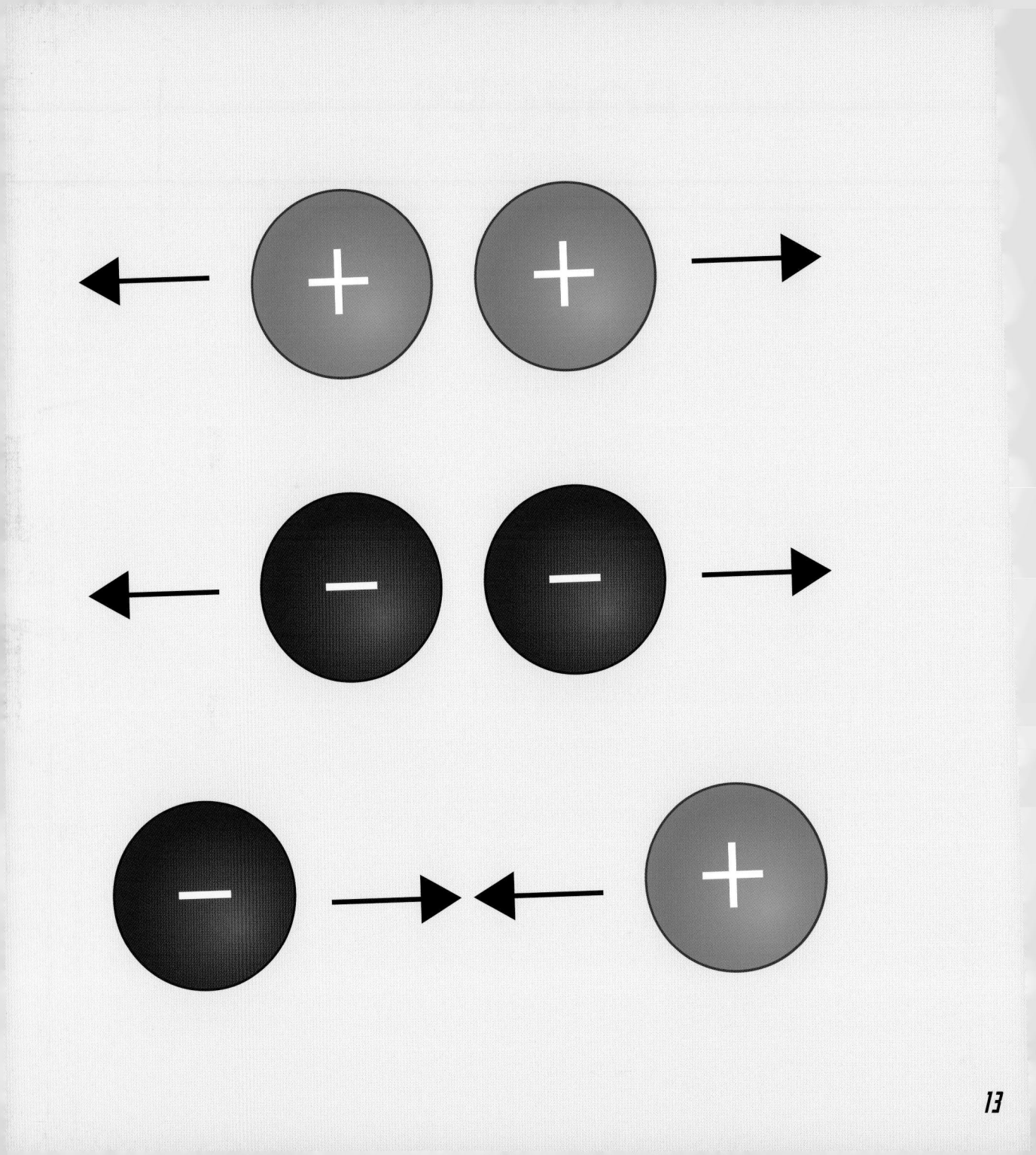

USING **FORCES**

We use forces all the time to move, work and play. Often, several forces act at once. A golfer hits a ball with a club. The club makes the ball go up. Gravity makes the ball come down. Friction makes the rolling ball slow down and stop.

Machines make our work easier so we use less force. Machines are made up of simple tools such as wheels, **_inclined planes_** and **_pulleys_**. It's hard to push a heavy box along the ground. When you put the box on a trolley with wheels, it moves much more easily. An inclined plane, such as a ramp, helps us to move a heavy box to a higher level. Builders use cranes with pulleys to lift heavy things even higher.

inclined plane slanting surface that is used to move objects to different levels
pulley grooved wheel turned by a rope, belt or chain that is used to move heavy objects

Wheels and inclined planes do more than help get heavy objects from one place to another. They also help people who can't walk. Wheelchairs and ramps help people to go upstairs without having to climb steps.

PUSHING
WITH THRUST

Thrust is a kind of pushing force. It is caused when **exhaust** moving in one direction pushes an object in the opposite direction. An aeroplane burns fuel and makes exhaust. The exhaust pushes out from the back of the aeroplane, making the plane move forward.

thrust force that pushes a vehicle forward
exhaust waste gases that come out of an engine

IT IS ROCKET SCIENCE!

How does a giant rocket fly all the way into space? Thrust! Huge amounts of burning rocket fuel make *energy*. This energy produces thrust, which pushes the rocket up. A rocket must carry enough fuel to push the rocket free of Earth's gravity.

energy ability to do work such as moving things or giving heat or light

19

FORCE **EXPERIMENT**

HOW FAR CAN YOU GO?

MATERIALS:

- plank of wood about 30 to 45 centimetres (12 to 18 inches) long and about 8 centimetres (3 inches) wide to use as a ramp
- long, smooth tabletop or floor
- 4 large plastic locking blocks
- toy car with moveable wheels
- tape measure
- tea towel
- rubber mat

WHAT TO DO: PART 1

1. Set up the ramp on one end of the table. Place one end of the wooden plank on top of one plastic block, with the other end resting on the table (or floor).

2. Place the car on top of the ramp and let it go. Use the tape measure to measure how far the car went before it stopped moving. Write down the answer.

3. Remove the ramp. Add one block on top of the first block, and replace the ramp. Repeat step 2.

4. Add the third block and repeat step 2 again.

5. What happens if you add a fourth block?

Did the height of the ramp affect the distance that the car went? Why?

WHAT TO DO: PART 2

1. Set up the ramp with two blocks under it.

2. Place the tea towel on the table with one end just under the low end of the ramp. The rest should be spread out along the table.

3. Place the car on top of the ramp and let it go. Use the tape measure to measure how far the car went before it stopped moving.

4. Replace the tea towel with the rubber mat. Repeat step 2 again.

On which surface did the car go further? Did either of the surfaces let the car go further than the two-block ramp on the smooth table? Why?

GLOSSARY

atoms tiny particles (pieces) of which everything is made

energy ability to do work such as moving things or giving heat or light

exhaust waste gases that come out of an engine

friction force made when two objects rub against each other; friction slows down objects

inclined plane slanting surface that is used to move objects to different levels

pulley grooved wheel turned by a rope, belt or chain that is used to move heavy objects

resistance force that opposes or slows the motion of an object; friction is a form of resistance

surface outside or outermost area of something

thrust force that pushes a vehicle forward

FIND OUT MORE

BOOKS

Forces and Motion (Essential Physical Science), Angela Royston (Raintree, 2014)

Science Encyclopedia, Kirsteen Robson (Usborne Publishing, 2015)

When Forces and Motion Collide (Engage Literacy), Chris Oxlade (Raintree, 2017)

WEBSITES

www.bbc.com/education/topics/zvpp34j
Learn more about pushes and pulls!

www.dkfindout.com/uk/science/forces-and-motion
Find out more about forces and motion.

COMPREHENSION QUESTIONS

1. What are the two main things forces do?

2. Name three types of forces.

3. Choose one simple tool we use and explain how it decreases a person's use of force.

INDEX

atoms 12

friction 8, 9

gravity 10, 11, 19

machines 16
movement 6, 8, 9, 12, 14, 16,
        18, 19

particles 12

resistance 9

speed 6

thrust 18, 19

weight 10, 11